Japanese Canadian Journey

Journey

The Nakagama Story

N. Rochelle Yamagishi

All photos supplied by the Nakagama family. Fiftieth anniversary photo by Lorne Kemmet Photography

Preliminary cover concept by Kendra Nakagama, Ryutaro Nakagama's granddaughter

Order this book online at www.trafford.com
or email orders@trafford.com

Most Trafford titles are also available at major online book retailers.

Printed in Victoria, BC, Canada.

ISBN: 978-1-4269-2937-3

Our mission is to efficiently provide the world's finest, most comprehensive book publishing service, enabling every author to experience success. To find out how to publish your book, your way, and have it available worldwide, visit us online at www.trafford.com

Trafford rev. 05/13/2010

 www.trafford.com

North America & international
toll-free: 1 888 232 4444 (USA & Canada)
phone: 250 383 6864 ✦ fax: 812 355 4082

PREFACE

Rochelle Yamagishi's *Japanese Canadian Journey: The Nakagama Story* is about a period in Canadian history that is still not well understood. Ostensibly, the book is about Ryutaro Nakagama, who left a small fishing village in southern Japan in 1924 to build a new life in a land that was sometimes reluctant to embrace him.

But while the narration of one Japanese-Canadian's personal struggle is interesting and sometimes even inspiring, the book speaks from the heart on another level. It shines a light on one of the darker chapters of Canadian history, the treatment of Japanese-Canadians before, during, and immediately after the Second World War.

I connect with *Japanese Canadian Journey* in a personal way in that it has helped me to make sense out of a puzzling childhood experience. As a child I was fortunate to be able to spend my summers with my grandparents in a small British Columbia mining town, Britannia Town Site. The mine closed in the early 60's and the town closed down as well, though a sister community, Britannia Beach, still exists in a fashion astride the highway from Vancouver to Whistler. Halfway between the two towns, at the upper terminus of the cable car line, was the ghost town of my childhood.

Until the spring of 1942 this had been a vibrant Japanese-Canadian community, alive with the laughter of mothers, fathers, and children. The men worked either in the copper mine or in related labouring jobs, while many of the women supplemented their family income by doing laundry or domestic work at either of the two Britannias.

That world came to an end suddenly in the spring of 1942. As difficult as it was for Japanese-Canadians elsewhere to pack for an uncertain future, you can imagine what it must have been like when the only way out of town was by an open cable car. Looking at the abandoned community through a child's eyes, I tried to imagine the pain, the confusion, the senselessness of it all. *Japanese Canadian Journey* helps me to understand the personal story of the evacuation, because it was at its heart a personal story.

There is, of course, another dimension to *Japanese Canadian Journey*. Like many great books, it is about persistence, endurance, survival, and dignity. That Ryutaro Nakagama should have escaped poverty in Japan only to meet personal discrimination and government indifference is the stuff legends are made of. And in a quiet way, his story is a legend. Nakagama never appeared on the national stage but within his community he was known as a persistent, hard-working, innovative businessman who could be taken at his word. And within his family and the circle of his friends, he was respected as a loving man who exhibited courage, industry, modesty, and respect for others. Part of his legacy is that the business he created in 1947 is still thriving today.

In one sense, though, you might make the case that *Japanese Canadian Journey* is not about Ryutaro Nakagama at all. Part of the richness of Yamagishi's book is that it stands for those many Japanese Canadian men and women who refused to be defeated or embittered by circumstance.

And we are a better community and a better nation because they prevailed.

Domo Arigato, Ryutaro Nakagama!

Robert D. Tarleck (signature)

Robert D. (Bob) Tarleck, M.A., M.Ed.
Ako'Tasi (Blackfoot for Man with Many Horses)
Mayor, City of Lethbridge

RDT/dgs

ACKNOWLEDGEMENTS

The original impetus for this book came from a Glenbow Museum exhibit called, "Mavericks," which opened in Calgary, AB in 2007. The Nikkei Cultural Society of Lethbridge and Area was asked for the name of an outstanding Japanese Canadian to feature in the exhibit. The Education Committee of the NCS gathered to discuss the request, and at first, decided that it was not culturally acceptable for one person to be so named, since it is a Japanese cultural precept that no one should stick out, or rise above the crowd, for recognition. ("Japaneseness" is a sense of belonging to the group, and for the good of the whole group.) However, since the Glenbow focus was on individuals, Japanese Canadians as a group could not be represented in the Mavericks exhibit. The Committee therefore convened again, and after some brainstorming, decided to approach the Nakagama family, in order to submit the name of the deceased Ryutaro Nakagama, as one Japanese person whose accomplishments had made him unique in the Japanese Canadian community in Alberta. Mrs. Nakagama was approached by her family and after some discussion, she gave her consent for the family story to be disseminated. Due to limitation of space in the Glenbow exhibit, however, only a small portion of the story could be told. Therefore, I have undertaken to present the story in its entirety in this volume.

I am grateful first to Mr. Ryutaro Nakagama, for his vision, mission, and perseverance in meeting the needs of his fellow Japanese Canadians. He realized that they needed familiar "comfort foods," having emigrated from Japan in the early 1900s, and then being forcibly removed from their second homes in British Columbia, to the alien terrain and demanding work of the sugar beets fields in southern Alberta. Secondly, my humble gratitude goes to Mrs. Nakagama, for giving her permission, and having the courage--along with other members of the family--to share the family story and photos. Since her English is limited, and my Japanese is virtually non-existent, I was grateful to be able to work with members of the Nakagama family, and in particular, to three of them, for their willingness to delve deeply into their individual and collective memories for the family stories, timelines, and photos: eldest daughter, Rita Aoki, (and her son, Darren, who suggested paragraph titles), third daughter, Carol Tomomitsu, and only son, Ken Nakagama (and his daughter, Kendra, who created the preliminary cover design), and their families. I appreciated them taking the time to record their memories, meet with me, discuss possibilities, and share ideas. Their dedication, to representing the family and the story respectfully, and as accurately as possible, was admirable. We realized, as a group, that we needed to cooperate, to work through memories and stories, in order to make sense of individual recollections and reminiscences that are, understandably, subject to lapses and distortions over time.

Another thank you to those who undertook the tasks of editing and proofreading, in addition to members of the Nakagama family: Mayor Bob Tarleck and Ruth Oltmann. In addition, the support of Michelle Lang and Ron Ulrich was appreciated. In the background, were my own family members, always interested and supportive, and cheering me on from the sidelines.

The Nikkei Cultural Society of Lethbridge and Area has graciously supported this work financially, and in spirit, in order to help carry out its mandate of sharing the Japanese culture in Southern Alberta, for those of Japanese descent and others, alike. I am grateful for the positive response to my previous book, *Nikkei Journey: Japanese Canadians in Southern Alberta* (2005). I am told that its stories helped to articulate a post-war history in southern Alberta that had previously been silenced, while Japanese Canadians strove to better themselves through education and hard work, in order to overcome the shame of their forced removal ["evacuation"] from the west coast of Canada, after the bombing of Pearl Harbor in 1941, during World War II. I hope that this work will continue to inform and inspire.

DEDICATION

To the Japanese Canadians in southern Alberta: "all my relations," a phrase and concept that has been borrowed from Native American ideology, the belief that humans are all in an "intimate kinship" with one another, and that we must live and work together in harmony, in order to live peaceably together on this earth.

And to my precious mother, Faith Yayeko (Adachi) Sato [1924-1984], who might have gone to teacher's college, had it not been for the events of World War II. She faithfully read to us when we were young, and shared her love of literature with all her children.

N.R.Y.
Calgary, AB 23 February 2010

CHAPTER 1

Emigration

It is believed that the first Japanese immigrant to Canada was Manzo Nagano. Only 19 years old, he landed in New Westminster, British Columbia in 1877. However, when his ship returned to the Orient, for whatever reason, he was not on board. He spent the next 46 years in British Columbia, engaging in various occupations—fisherman, longshoreman, and businessman. Many Japanese immigrants followed him, in both emigration and work patterns in later years.

By 1885, immigration to Canada had increased from a small trickle to a steady flow. From 1897 to 1901, more than 15,000 Japanese arrived in Canadian ports. Many of them were transients who were only looking for seasonal work, and then returned home, or moved on to the United States. The 1901 census recorded nearly 5,000 Japanese actually living in Canada, many of whom had entered from 1885 to 1900.

The majority of the early immigrants consisted of those from peasant class farming and fishing villages in the southern parts of Japan. Due to famines and floods, and overpopulation, they were desperate to find a new labour market. Typically, an emigrant from Japan was young, single, and male, with little money and no knowledge of the English language. He bravely set off for a totally foreign land, with little more than his hopes, ambitions and a high level of energy.

In a similar way to emigration patterns from Europe, people who were looking for a new start set sail for the "New World." People with individualistic ways were considered misfits in Japanese culture, which emphasized rigidity, cooperation, belonging, and group thinking. It was only logical for them to move to the city, or to emigrate.

Ryutaro Nakagama comes to Canada

"My father, Ryutaro Nakagama, was born on December 9, 1906 in Makurazaki, Kagoshima-ken. His parents, my grandparents, Iwataro and Kisa Nakagama, already had a son and daughter, Tsunetaro and Miye, respectively. They all lived in a small fishing village on the southern tip of Japan. In Japanese culture, the first son is the one who had the familial obligation to take over the family farm, and to produce heirs to carry on the family name. It was no surprise then that my grandfather gave consent to my father, the second son, to move to Canada.

"Young and single at the time, my father, Ryutaro, viewed his move to Canada as a new adventure, a chance to break away from existing conditions in his homeland. Reminiscing in later life, he often spoke of the poverty in Japan, including going to school barefoot and having only a roasted yam for lunch. In his village of Makurazaki, which is still known for the production of *katsuobushi*, made from dried bonito fish, Ryutaro would probably have continued with the family, in fishing work in some form, with his father and brother. My father had completed high school in Japan, but he had no formal training beyond that."

"Ryutaro Nakagama, at age 20 when he became a naturalized Canadian citizen on October 2, 1926."

"Luckily for me, my father had been born after 1867, when the rule of the Emperor was restored. Prior to that, under the control of the powerful Tokugawa warrior family, Japan had been a rigidly closed society for 200 years. The Emperor started to advocate studying abroad, and two decades later, lifted a ban against overseas emigration of labourers. If my father had never left Japan, I would not be able to tell you the remarkable story of his emigration and enterprise in Canada. It is ironic that it is precisely because he was *not* the firstborn son that I, many many years later, *as* his firstborn son, have been able to carry on his legacy in southern Alberta, Canada."

"Miye & Chosaburo Nakagama, who sponsored Ryutaro's immigration to Canada in 1924, to work in the fishing industry at Steveston, B.C."

"On April 16, 1924, the 18-year-old Ryutaro arrived in Victoria, British Columbia on the *S.S. McKinley*. His older sister, my aunt Miye, and her husband, Chosaburo Nakagama (no relation) had emigrated earlier, and sponsored my father to work in Steveston, B.C. My Uncle Chosaburo had his own fishing boat and fishing license, under which the two men could fish, so my father worked with his brother-in-law in the fishing industry for three years, from 1924 to 1927. Typically, Japanese immigrants at the beginning of the 20th century came to Canada only temporarily, to seek their fortune in the "land of gold," but there was no indication of this goal for my father. He seemed intent on staying in Canada to make his future. The decision was confirmed when he became a naturalized Canadian citizen on October 2, 1926."

Most Japanese immigration was facilitated by private contractors, rather than the Canadian government, which did no solicitation in Japan, as it had in Europe and the British Isles. However, intrigued by the prospect of an overseas adventure, young Japanese men were able to sign up with private contractors who came to their local villages. In the wave of emigration from Japan, most of the immigrants came from the villages in southern Japan—especially the prefectures of Wakayama, Shiga, Kagoshima, and Hiroshima. They were mostly poor farmers, fishermen, or small merchants, and the immigrants usually followed the same occupations in Canada: the fishermen from Wakayama settled in the fishing village of Steveston, and the farmers in the Fraser Valley and the Okanagan, all in British Columbia. The commercial traders and farmers, from Shiga and Kagoshima, set up small business ventures in Vancouver, or on farms in the Fraser and Okanagan Valleys.

CHAPTER 2

Immigration Policies and Practices

From 1885 to 1909, most Japanese immigrants were single males, all hoping to make quick fortunes within a few years, and then return to the home of their ancestors. In North America, people of the labouring class found opportunities that were closed to them in Japan. The emigrants were sent off by hopeful relatives, with the directive to come back home as soon as possible "with your golden clothes," or, "dressed in brocade." Little did they know that life was very different from what they had been led to believe, and as a result, the first immigrants found that they would have to stay longer to complete those plans, if they would be able to meet their initial goals at all. Many chose to remain in Canada, forging a different path for their new lives.

The majority of early Japanese immigrants had found their way to Canada through private contracting companies, with contacts in Canada, who had sent agents to the various districts of Japan to solicit emigrants. Part of their strategy was to obtain financial security from their relatives, to guarantee compliance with the requirements. The company managed all the details and practicalities of emigration, so that the prospective emigrant only had to apply to the Japanese government for a three-year passport, and undergo scrutiny by the local police authorities. Once they arrived in Canada, they were required to register with the Japanese consul, although the passport time limit was not strictly enforced. The companies collected commission for their services from all emigrants, including the cost of a return trip, in case of sickness or financial need. However, the favourable living and working conditions in Canada were often greatly exaggerated, in an effort to encourage people to commit themselves to the venture. In addition to advertising in newspapers, there were circulars and pamphlets sent out to the villages, as a means of inducement to sign up.

Japanese immigrants, once in Canada, stayed close together in groups, at work, and living in their own communities. They often did not learn to speak English, since they were grouped together under a Japanese "boss," who acted as their interpreter with the employer. In the fishing village of Steveston at this time, the entire population was Japanese and there was no need to learn English.

During this period in history, cheap labour was in high demand in Canada, and the young Japanese seemed to fill the bill, with their physical agility, quickness with their hands, physical fitness, and resilient temperaments. With little more than the clothes on their backs, their physical strength, natural wit, and ambition, they arrived in Canada, eager to work. Since many of them were from the lower social strata, they had had to borrow funds for their ocean passage, from relatives and friends. Feeling a great sense of obligation, they had expected to quickly repay their debts, through frugal living and hard work. In order to meet their debts, they lived a lifestyle similar to that in the homeland, lacking physical comforts. They bunked in crowded quarters with their fellow workmen, in logging and railway camps, and near the fishing canneries. In the winter, they would move to the cities, such as Vancouver, staying in crowded boarding houses, in order to save as much money as possible, with the idea of returning to Japan as soon as possible. They would send money back to parents and family, and sometimes to wives and children.

CHAPTER 3

Japanese Settlement on the West Coast of Canada

The steady stream of new arrivals from Japan into Steveston, to become fishermen, was a serious concern for both the White and Native Indian fishermen, who already dominated the fishing industry there. In 1893, in order to maintain their hold, these two groups combined forces, to demand a government-sponsored reduction of fishing licenses issued to the Japanese. In 1900, a confrontation between the groups required the militia to be brought in, to protect strikebreakers who were willing to fish, and to avert mass violence. The White fishermen organized themselves as the B.C. Fishermen's Union, but since they would not allow the Japanese to join, the Japanese formed their own association. With the support of British Columbia politicians, the B.C. Fishermen's Union lobbied the Department of Marine and Fisheries of the federal government, resulting in a ceasing of additional licenses being issued to Japanese Canadian fishermen in 1919. A fisheries commission was set up, to enquire into the Pacific Coast fishing situation. In 1923, Ottawa revoked 40 per cent of gillnet licenses issued to Japanese Canadians and called for a further reduction of ten per cent each year, in an attempt to eliminate the problematic Japanese fishermen, who seemed to be more successful than their predecessors. The Japanese Canadian fishermen's organization went to the Supreme Court of Canada for a decision in 1928, and obtained a ruling that the government did not have the power to deny a license to any Canadian citizen. By that time, however, about half of all the *Nikkei* (people of Japanese descent) fishermen had left the industry for other occupations, or even returned to Japan.

By 1901, the Japanese held 1,958 fishing licenses out of a total of 4,722 issued in the province of British Columbia. With two men to a boat or license, that could mean that there were about 4,000 Japanese involved in the fishing industry. Most of these fishermen lived in Steveston and worked in the waters in that area, but later migrated up the coast to the Naas and Skeena Rivers. In 1899, the village of Steveston was populated with about 2,000 Japanese. The community had built its own hospital, just in time to meet the needs of many numbers of fishermen who became victims of a typhoid epidemic.

Steveston was home to about 1,800 members of the Japanese Fishermen's Association, the forerunner of the Amalgamated Association of Fishermen. Japanese fishermen worked hard, and became very successful at their work, developing a salting process for salmon and herring, in order to export it in huge shipments to Japan. Japanese fishermen and Whites competed over the prices given to them by the canneries, precipitating violent incidents that were precursors to the Riot of 1907, which erupted on the streets of Vancouver. Responding to the wave of anti-Japanese sentiment, the British Columbia government appealed to Ottawa, resulting in Ottawa arranging with Japan to restrict immigration, beginning a pattern of the two authorities working together to address what was called, the "Oriental problem."

CHAPTER 4

Early Racial Strife in B.C.

In the province of British Columbia, over a period of 70 years, an Anti-Asian movement looked upon the Japanese, along with other Asians—Chinese and East Indians—as not only inferior, but culturally inassimilable to the Canadian way of life and to British values and institutions. These people were therefore systematically excluded from the social and institutional life of their larger communities. In response, the Japanese Canadians formed their own small communities, in order to supply their own social, cultural, and economic institutions. As the Japanese became more concentrated in their own communities, and were able to preserve the Japanese family styles and customs, they became more visible as a group, and unwittingly increased the prejudice against them. Ironically, since they were not allowed to participate fully in the dominant culture, they clung to their cultural ways, which only accentuated their predicted lack of assimilation. However, based on the Japanese culture of the homeland, they placed great importance on group belonging, promoting harmony, industry and frugality, and in the process also controlled crime and delinquency in their communities.

A geographical area in Vancouver—centred on Powell Street—became the focal point of Japanese activities. It was well-developed by the early 1900s, and known as "Little Tokyo." It included cafes, dry goods stores, food stores, ice cream parlours, pool halls, barbers, dry cleaners, garages, fish markets, Japanese-language school and community hall, baseball sandlot, Buddhist temple, and Christian churches. Japanese people enjoyed chatting with each other in their native tongue, creating a miniature community that mimicked the life that they had left in Japan, a kind of compensation for the unfulfilled dream of returning to Japan.

Although initially intended as a colony of British landholders, British Columbia was unable to exclude the "wrong" (i.e., non-white) settlers, due to the necessity for labourers. In 1858, gold strikes on the Fraser River attracted large numbers of Chinese from California. Similar to the Japanese, they were regarded as "undesirable and inassimilable" by the White population, but temporarily accepted, and only for the purposes of menial and/or dangerous labour. In 1881, when construction began on the Canadian Pacific Railway, with a plan to complete the route to the west coast, thousands of Chinese labourers were imported, marking a burgeoning of the "Oriental problem" in British Columbia. Although the Japanese and Chinese were often lumped together by non-whites, as if they were one "amorphous, inscrutable mass," the Japanese had hardly any relations with the Chinese, and had always considered themselves a separate entity from them, as from other ethnic groups. Although the two groups are undoubtedly genetically similar, they are strikingly different in cultural terms. For example, the Chinese were comparatively indifferent to the political and economic discrimination, which was bitterly resented and resisted by the Japanese.

"Mary, youngest Nakagama daughter, dressed in a kimono, standing in front of the first Japanese store in Lethbridge, AB, which Ryutaro opened on rental premises in October 1947."

Oriental connections

"When my father established his first store in Lethbridge, Alberta, he was obliged to remain on the outskirts of the city, in an area that was, ironically, also home to the Chinese, who were similarly placed on the margins, geographically and socially. In both of our store locations, we carried out our businesses side-by-side, with the Chinese families, who also usually lived above or adjacent to their stores. As a result, our family members became close personal friends of the Chinese. My best friends were the Dong children. There were five of them altogether--three boys and two girls--and we

15

all attended elementary school together. The same holds true for my older sisters, who were closer in age to the Leong family."

In the late 1800s, the provincial government attempted to stop immigration of any more Orientals, and also restrict their employment. Employers were happy with the cheaper wages that Japanese workers would accept, due to their poorer living conditions, although their White competitors for jobs in the working class complained bitterly at the low wages. Although the Japanese were seen as adaptable to the Canadian mode of dress and living style, they were also seen to fall easily into the White man's vices, of drinking and gambling.

Ryutaro's views on gambling

"Dad enjoyed his beer, but gambling was something that my father did not tolerate. He made a point to stress this within the family. I remember when I was about six years old, playing 'Old Maid' with a friend, and my father took the cards away. It was a few years later that he explained his strict views. He remembered acquaintances who would gamble for hours and hours, sometimes for the whole day, and he thought that this was an inexcusable waste of one's time. He had known a few acquaintances who had lost almost everything they owned, to gambling. He did later travel to places like Las Vegas, and of course played the slot machines, but his point was that you could play these games for entertainment and a temporary distraction, but it was unwise to get into the habit of gambling all the time. He felt strongly that people should find something better to do with their free time.

"My parents expected that their children should

always strive for personal excellence in whatever
they did, but they should never become boastful
or take excessive pride in their achievements or
possessions. Japanese people of their generation
never openly displayed their emotions, so expres-
sions of love and praise were rarely bestowed on
family members. It may have been that they believed it was a method of discipline to withhold
their pride and happiness at their children's accomplishments, which would keep them from becoming boastful or proud."

People from the Far East experienced overt hostility
towards them, being so easily distinguishable from other
immigrants and the dominant White group in British
Columbia. Coupled with a Japanese cultural value of
strong dedication to the group, and Japanese values and
ethical codes, the feeling of separateness was intensified.
However, despite huge differences in language, physical
characteristics, ceremonial customs and etiquette, family
relationships, food habits and cultural values, the Japanese
as a group were the object of attempts at conversion to
Christianity, and many Japanese saw Christianity as a way
for them to identify more closely with White society.

A Christian mission was established in Victoria and a
Sunday School in Vancouver, guided by a minister from
Seattle, Washington, who was sent to work among the
fishermen in Skeena. Supported by the larger Protestant
denominations in Canada, outreach projects came to
realization, such as a Methodist church built in Vancouver
in 1906, at the corner of Jackson and Powell. However,
the Buddhist immigrants not only lacked funds for the
infrastructure to meet their religious needs, but also had
to struggle to reconstruct their old faith in Canada. The
first Buddhist temple in Canada was opened in 1905 in
Vancouver, with a priest brought over from Japan.

Remarkably, the money that built the temple came from the meager earnings of the labourers who gave to the cause as they could. Moreover, whenever life crises arose, such as weddings and funerals, families tended to revert to their customary ancestral worship patterns and rituals, reinforcing the Japanese culture and ethical code. The transplanting of Buddhism to Canada resulted in the development of a strange mix of both Christian and Buddhist customs and features, so that the temples came to be called "churches" and the priests "ministers."

Steveston was a self-contained fishing village occupied mainly by Japanese, and most businesses--dry goods and hardware, fabric, clothing and shoe stores, a barbershop, bakery, confectionery store, etc.--were operated by Japanese, except for the hotel and regulated essential services, such as bank, hospital, post office, etc. There were two grocery stores that carried Japanese groceries, dry foods, and staples, such as rice, *shoyu*, and *miso*.

Ryutaro's spirituality as part of his business dealings

"Although my father was a member of the Buddhist Church, he was not a regular attender, nor was he very much involved with church activities or social organizations, other than *judo*. My father often talked about the art, its philosophy, and how its tenets could be incorporated into daily living.

"In 1937, he earned his black belt in *judo* in Steveston. Traditional Japanese values were also a subject of frequent conversation, such as walking the 'straight path,' giving your best personal effort to all endeavours, and not giving in to failure. He often talked to me about applying fairness and integrity in all business dealings and giving recognition and respect for the support and help he had received from others. Despite losses in life, or business setbacks, he tried to follow his vision for business success, applying *judo* teachings to maintain strength in body and spirit. Family members fondly remember his advice to them: 'Whatever you do in life, try to be the best, and even if you end up a dishwasher, be the best.'

"Besides his interest in *judo*, my father was interested in *kendo* and *aikido*, less well-known Japanese martial arts. He would love to talk about *aikido* and demonstrate various techniques. It was a difficult sport to learn, because of the limited resources in Canada, but he studied and learned about *aikido* by reading books from Japan. He liked *aikido* because of its philosophy: using the power of the opponents against themselves, passive power as opposed to active power, like *judo*, but there are no direct strikes or hits. Before he became ill near the end of his life, he passed on a copy of an *aikido* book to other family members.

"Although Ryutaro had actually transplanted himself from one fishing village to another, each on different sides of the Pacific Ocean, he actually disliked fishing work, and instead had a dream to open a store in Steveston, to sell fresh fish. The population of Steveston, comprised of Japanese people, socialized together within their groups-- with personal and work friends, clubs/organizations such as *judo, kendo,* church activities, etc. With the large population of Japanese in Steveston, it must have seemed like a ready market for Japanese-style foods.

"It is interesting to consider the historical events that preceded my father's arrival in Canada, and which ultimately led to his decision to open a business in Steveston. Having only self-taught skills needed to operate and develop a business, my father began on a small scale, with his first venture being a peddling service to Steveston residences. Service to his customers was always foremost in his business plans, and in 1927, he began manually pulling an open cart, called a *dai-hachi kuruma,* filled with wares, such as gloves, boots, and aprons, needed for cannery work. Most women in Steveston worked every day in the canneries, and therefore they did not have time or opportunity to go shopping. The customers began to request fresh vegetables and fruits, and other such items that he could carry to the homes. As he went along, Ryutaro taught himself about food management and the handling of fresh foods, fish, and meat. In 1928, he opened his first storefront business on rented premises on Moncton Street in Steveston. Although one of many other stores in the community, his was the first to sell fresh fish, which was otherwise not available in local waters, but which had to be brought in from Vancouver.

"He also sold other Japanese foods, and eventually added fresh meat products. Tuna, mackerel, squid, and octopus were popular with the Japanese, but not yet available in the Steveston retail market. Other inventory included fresh vegetables, such as *nappa* (Chinese cabbage), *daikon* (Japanese radish), cabbage, celery, onions, and fresh products, such as *age* (deep-fried soybean cakes) and *tofu* (soybean cake), some canned goods, and dried *udon* (Japanese-style noodles). He supplied specialty products, rather than the basic staples for Japanese cooking, such as rice, *shoyu* (soy sauce), *miso* (soy bean paste for making soup), as these were available from neighbouring stores."

"Post-war photograph of Moncton Street in Steveston, B.C., where Ryutaro opened his first storefront business in 1928 on rental premises. In the spring of 1941, one year prior to evacuation, he purchased the meat store across the street."

Travelling to "Little Tokyo"

"In 'Japan Town' (or 'Little Tokyo'), around the area of Cordova and Powell Streets of Vancouver, Japanese businessmen manufactured soy sauce and *miso*. (Some of these companies—such as Amano—are still in business today.) Every morning, my father would drive his truck into the city of Vancouver to obtain fresh fish, *tofu*, vegetables, and groceries, from wholesale and retail outlets on Powell Street in Vancouver. Most of his customers from Steveston had no vehicles of their own, and were often given rides in the truck, from Steveston into Vancouver, for shopping and personal business. The truck was usually full of passengers, on a daily basis."

*Ryutaro Nakagama with Harry Tanigami, one of the young clerks who
helped in the Steveston stores, taking orders and making home deliveries.
They are standing in front of the truck in which daily trips were made
into Vancouver, B.C. to purchase fish and fresh food products.*

CHAPTER 5

Family Building Phase for Japanese Immigrants

After the immigrants had worked in Canada for much longer than they had originally intended, married men sent back to Japan for their wives and families, and single men sent for "picture brides." As was traditional, families and friends arranged marriages, even though they were far way in the homeland. The relatives of the immigrants sought out a suitable woman in their own, or a neighbouring, village or prefecture (province). The prospective couple then exchanged photographs. Photo studios were set up in "Little Tokyo" on Powell Street in Vancouver, where a man could don a borrowed three-piece suit and top hat, and pose for his picture, which would be printed on a postcard to send to Japan. No doubt, at the receiving end in Japan, these contrived photos resulted in confirming the widespread belief that North America was a land of opportunity.

Arranged marriages were still a feature of society in Japan, so extrapolating to Canada was not a big adaptation. Family alliances, rather than romantic courtship, were more important features of the process. Once the members of the prospective couple agreed to the union, the immigrant would declare his intentions by writing to his relatives, and the marriage would be registered in Japan. The bride and groom would exchange letters, the groom would arrange for a passport, and then the woman would come to Canada, usually several months later, as his wife. These proxy marriages usually worked well, due to cultural similarities in the bride and groom. They also fulfilled an important function at the time. Entering the marriage with the understanding of being helpmates to each other, the new couple struggled to adjust to life in the new country. The prospective bride likely did not have a realistic idea of the life she were to lead in Canada, but she might have agreed to the tremendous change in lifestyle as a way to seek adventure, and to avoid the complex web of indebtedness to parents—in particular the mother-in-law—that was typically an onerous requirement in marriage in Japanese society. The woman virtually married the family, rather than the man, submitting to a circle of obligations and restraints that severely constricted her life. The picture brides began to arrive in 1908, adapting quickly to the new Canadian culture, and starting families, once they were in Canada.

In this "family-building" phase, during the 1920s, about one-third of the 15,868 Japanese in Canada were female, with the birth rate of Canadian-born *(Nisei)* totaling 4,334. During this period, anti-Oriental pressures lessened somewhat, and Japanese settlements began to become more permanent in nature. Primitive communities of the past changed in character into self-sufficient ghettos, with their own network of institutions, shops, schools, churches, restaurants, mutual aid and prefectural societies. There was also more stability provided when people began to move into occupations and businesses that promised a more secure future, rather than relying on the whims of the White employers.

The efforts of the first immigrants paved the way for later arrivals, likely increasing opportunities for their children, compared to what they might have had in the home country. The characteristic Japanese spirit of mutual helpfulness, and sense of obligation, often led to the actions of helping new arrivals—especially those coming from the same area in Japan--to establish themselves in their new country. Since people from the same prefecture were drawn together by the common bond of local customs and dialect, many lived close together and worked together, or in similar types of jobs. The Okinawans, although not originally a Japanese group, but lumped together with them by the Americans after World War II, moved to the coal mining areas around Hardieville and Lethbridge, in southern Alberta, best demonstrating this prevailing pattern of togetherness.

"Family and friends holding streamers, connected with loved ones and passengers aboard a ship departing for Japan. As the ship departed, the paper streamers would break, in farewell. On this occasion, Ryutaro and Nobuko, with infant daughter, are bidding farewell to Nobuko's brother, Hideo, who is sailing to meet his future bride, arranged through bai-shakunin, as had his sister, Nobuko's marriage."

My parents' marriage

"When my grandmother became ill and passed away, as the oldest daughter, my mother was then obliged to stay with the remaining family in Canada, and a few years later, to marry my father. Before her marriage, my mother had worked in a Vancouver dry cleaning operation as a seamstress, during the years 1934 to 1937. As was the Japanese tradition even in Canada, her father arranged for her marriage to a man from the same geographical area in Japan, in this case, my father, Ryutaro Nakagama. *Bai-shakunin* or 'go-between'--one representative for each partner—usually made the official decision for the marriage, although in this particular case, only one *bai-shakunin* acted as a go-between on behalf of both partners. When the *bai-shakunin* first went to my mother's house to pursue the idea of marriage, my mom actually refused two times to entertain the idea, and did not want any discussion to take place involving marriage. I am happy to say that she relented later, whereupon the arrangements were made for marriage.

"The serving tray or betrothal gift--called y*uino,* and containing traditional items that were symbolic of good luck in the marriage –was received from the prospective groom after the decision, and consent to marry was thereby finalized. What now seems strange and almost unbelievable to us in the next generation, it was not until after arrangements were settled for marriage that the couple even met for the first time. Ironically, now adhering to Western tradition, they went together to purchase the engagement ring in Vancouver, although they had not ever seen or spoken to each other previously.

"Their second meeting occurred when Ryutaro picked up the 'dowry' items in his truck, as had been pre-arranged. The dowry items were a bedroom suite and sewing machine, purchased in Vancouver by her father, for Nobuko to take to the marriage. The third meeting was the actual wedding day, on which my mother wore a Western-style wedding gown. During the first four years of marriage, the couple lived in a rental property."

"Ryutaro and Nobuko Nakagama, on their wedding day, December 6, 1937."

CHAPTER 6

Discrimination Events in the Early Part of the 20ᵗʰ Century

In the fall of 1937, there had been demands for a boycott of Japanese imports, and an embargo on exports to Japan, from Vancouver to Montreal. Many years previous to that, in the summer of 1916, the first group of Japanese had gone overseas to fight with the 209ᵗʰ Battalion, and at the end of the war, racial relations were relatively calm, with most of the immigrants staying in the coastal area of British Columbia. They worked successfully in fishing, mining, lumbering, railroad labouring, or farming in the Fraser Valley, until the coming of the Great Depression, and with it a sharpening of negative attitudes towards the Japanese in British Columbia, not only due to economic concerns, but also linked to Japan's foreign policy decisions regarding the invasion of China.

The B.C. Legislative Assembly set up the Board of Review in 1938, in order to investigate charges of illegal entry of Japanese to Canada. Recommendations were made: for all people of Japanese ancestry to carry identification cards, for Japanese-language schools to be closed, and for part of the Oriental population to be transferred to other provinces. Although these changes were beyond the Board's authority, they were eventually put into effect, through the War Measures Act in 1941.

Ryutaro's first store purchase

"Looking at the events of the time, it is actually surprising to me that my parents were married at that particular time in history. How my father thought he could maintain a business, and support a wife and possibly also a family, I'll never know. My parents, along with the general population of Japanese in Canada, somehow survived all this political turmoil. Oblivious to the upheaval that was soon to come, or perhaps pressing on, even in the face of possible adversity, in the spring of 1941, Ryutaro purchased the meat store and equipment across the street from his first (rental) store.

"In the year following purchasing and setting up the store, Ryutaro's store operation itself remained basically the same. The couple furnished the adjacent residence with new furniture and settled in, with their first-born, my sister, Ritsuko (Rita)."

CHAPTER 7

Issues of Civil Rights for Japanese Canadians

When, in 1939, Canada entered the European war, the issue of military service for *Nisei* was raised. Prime Minister Mackenzie King made an official announcement regarding military service by Japanese Canadian citizens, that: "citizens of Japanese ancestry be exempted from service," because of the "dangerous" situation caused by anti-Japanese hostility in British Columbia. It was deemed unthinkable to have White and *Nisei* youths training together in camp and living in barracks together. Public fears of subversive activities, in the event of war with Japan, prompted King to impose a compulsory registration of Japanese people in Canada. This was thought to be necessary as a starting point, to give an accurate picture of actual population figures. The RCMP was charged with the work of registration in March 1941, completed in August, three months before the outbreak of the Pacific war.

CHAPTER 8

"Enemy Alien" Status and Politics

In keeping with their cultural values of hard work, family togetherness, and dedication, by the 1940s, the Japanese began to realize a measure of economic success. However, from the perspective of the people in the dominant population group, they were highly visible as a people who were an economic threat. As a result, when the Pearl Harbor attack came, on December 7, 1941, they were quickly identified as a group that could be called "enemy aliens."

Immediately after Japan's surprise attack on Pearl Harbor, the federal government responded by impounding some 1,200 fishing boats, all owned or operated by naturalized Canadian citizens or *Nisei*. The 59 Japanese-language schools and three vernacular newspapers published in Vancouver were all closed, on the advice of the RCMP, as "precautionary measures." On December 7, Order-in-Council P.C. 9591 extended provisions of the Defense of Canada Regulations to require Japanese nationals to register by February 7, 1942, with the Registrar of Enemy Aliens. Since the outbreak of war in Europe in

1939, German and Italian aliens had been required to report regularly to the Registrar. On December 16, however, regardless of citizenship or place of birth, P.C. 9760 made it mandatory for the registration of all persons of Japanese origin in Canada.

CHAPTER 9

The Evacuation of Japanese Canadians from the West Coast

The bombing of Pearl Harbor was seen as "treacherous" and "sneaky," which only added to anti-Japanese sentiment in the province. Government authorities believed that the people of B.C. could only be appeased by an announcement of mass evacuation of the Japanese in February 1942. Established on March 4, 1942, the British Columbia Security Commission was charged with planning, supervising and directing the evacuation. Order-in-Council P.C. 1665 gave the Commission the power to make by-laws, hold property, enter into contracts and employ staff, including federal civil servants of any department. If the evacuees were unable to take any property with them, it was placed in the custody of the Custodian of Alien Property, as "a protective measure."

Within a mere 10 days, the Commission displaced some 2,500 people, mainly fishermen and their families, living along the upper coastline of Vancouver Island, as far north as Prince Rupert. The Hastings Park Exhibition Grounds in Vancouver was used as a "clearing station" or "assembly centre" to house the evacuees, until the Department of

National Defense could arrange for them to move outside the "protected area." Hurriedly-cleaned stables and cattle stalls of the Livestock Building eventually housed up to 4,000 Japanese. Under guard of the RCMP, during the month of March, 1,593 women and children were shipped to the Park, while men were moved directly to road camps in the interior of British Columbia and in Ontario.

The evacuation process, based on reasons of "national security" or "military necessity," expelled a group of people from a large area of the country, without hearings or trials, but merely on the grounds of racial ancestry. In the absence of public opposition at the time, the federal government was not required to defend or define publicly this revoking of all rights of citizenship. The event never developed into a nation-wide issue, although it was carried out over several months, and completed in October 1942.

In keeping with their cultural background and their development as a minority group in B.C., most Japanese did not resist the evacuation, but cooperated docilely with authorities. Cultural norms of duty, obligation, conformity, and obedience were the foundation for a lack of resistance. Also important was the Japanese cultural outlook, *shikata-ga-nai* (directly translated as, "It can't be helped", described as a rationalization that one's fate is beyond personal control), coupled with the desire of *Nisei* to prove that they were "true Canadians" by being loyal to the government.

Japanese homeowners, businessmen, farmers, and fishermen alike were all stripped of their property, which was later liquidated by the Custodian of Alien Property. According to Order-in-Council P.C. 1665 on March 4, all motor vehicles (including automobiles, trucks, motorcycles and trailers) were impounded at Hastings Park; Japanese people were also required to surrender any radios, firearms and cameras. Most of this property was sold without the consent of the owners. The fishing boats were directed through an order-in-council (P.C. 251, Jan. 13, 1942) to be put back in operation with non-Japanese crews; another order (P.C. 288, issued on the same day) authorized the disposal of some 1,100 boats and their equipment, having a value of between two and three million dollars, with little, if any, compensation ever given to the owners of these properties. In some cases, owners were sent a bill for storage costs that exceeded the original value of the property.

Numerically, there were 23,149 people of Japanese descent in Canada at the time of the Pearl Harbor attack. This amounted to less than one-fifth of one per cent of the total Canadian population, and 2.7 per cent of the population in the British Columbia. The 22,096 who lived in British Columbia, mostly resided along the coastal region west of the Cascade mountain range, which was designated as a "protected area." Over half--and the largest segment of the group (13,309 people)--were Canadian citizens by virtue of birth, and 2,930 were immigrants who had been born in Japan but had become naturalized citizens. Of the 5,564 Japanese nationals, most had resided in Canada for 25 to 40 years. Of these, 2,006 were women.

According to the mathematical calculations then, of the Japanese Canadians in British Columbia, only about 2,000 could logically be deemed "dangerous," due to their close connection to Japan, in that they were male Japanese nationals. However, most of them had demonstrated loyalty to Canada, having lived and worked in Canada for decades. Thousands of people had been uprooted, despised, and shunted off to "somewhere else," to address this questionable danger.

In point of fact, the majority of the immigrants, *Issei* (first-generation Japanese immigrants), were well into middle age and had worked hard to build up a business or livelihood in Canada, looking forward in a few years to a life of rest and retirement. The Canadian-born generation, the *Nisei*, were predominantly adolescents and young adults, and were "Canadian" in speech, dress and manner. Educated in the public schools of British Columbia, most of them were bilingual, in order to communicate with their parents at home. They had already been subjected to many forms of discrimination, as had their parents, but had a firm belief in democratic principles, and therefore the large majority went along peaceably with the evacuation orders.

By March 17, able-bodied Japanese nationals, numbering over 1,000, had been placed in road camps on the Hope-Princeton road, the North Thompson highway and the British Columbia-Alberta Jasper route. Separated from their families while in the camps, they had concerns for their families' welfare and their loss of property, as well as inadequate medical attention, poor quality of food, and lack of privacy. In July, the Security Commission announced the possibility for men in road camps to be reunited with their families, due to expansion of housing facilities in the ghost towns of the interior of B.C.

By the spring of 1943, at peak occupation, these internment camps held 12,177 men, women and children, required to live under primitive and austere conditions and facing an unknown future. It was impossible to place groups of Japanese into larger cities in the interior of B.C., since their citizens violently opposed the relocation of Japanese to their city, despite serious labour shortages in their orchards and farms. Each camp was guarded by a detachment of the RCMP, which controlled traffic in and out of the camps. The rugged terrain and isolation of the camps, however, made it unnecessary to set up barbed wire or watchtowers. Each person of Japanese racial descent, over the age of 16, had been issued a registration card, containing a serial number, thumbprint and photograph. The card was to be carried at all times, a regulation that was kept in force until January 23, 1947. Travel was restricted, unless a permit was obtained from the RCMP or a Security Commission officer.

CHAPTER 10

Mid-War Developments

The British Columbia Security Commission, in responding to a labour shortage in the sugar beet fields in southern Alberta, offered the Japanese families as potential workers. The sugar beet growers readily agreed, viewing the Japanese as a readily exploitable group of people, since they would not be able to organize labour unions. Once the first Japanese people began to arrive in the province, however, public opposition began to build, leading to outcries from the Beet Workers' Union, city and labour councils, local Canadian Legion branches, boards of trade, and citizens' committees throughout southern Alberta. They demanded that Japanese from British Columbia not be admitted to the province, but if they were admitted, that they be guarded by the army and required to move from the province immediately after the war. British Columbia was accused of simply exporting its problem of the "Japanese menace" to Alberta. Alberta was the only province that demanded a written promise from the federal government to remove the displaced Japanese from the province at the end of the war.

CHAPTER 11

Southern Alberta Evacuation Story

On March 28, 1942, the sugar beet program was first announced, in which it was stated that 1,000 families would be moved to Alberta and Manitoba, each family to be given "individual cottages and small plots of land for its own use and cultivation" and assured of at least $1,000 for the season. This offer was an attractive alternative to some Japanese, who were relieved to be able to keep their families together, with this move. They were promised fair wages, free housing, public school education of the children, and welfare and medical services. Because Albertans did not want an uncontrolled influx of "inassimilable" Japanese people to their province, the Security Commission made a formal agreement with the Social Credit government of Alberta on May 6, promising absolute control over the Japanese moving into the area. In effect, the evacuees would be "frozen" to the farms to which they were assigned, blocking them from settling in the major cities such as Lethbridge, Edmonton or Calgary, or even small towns like Taber and Picture Butte, where they could become economic competitors with urban merchants.

Although the Japanese people did not anticipate that they would get rich, and many families did not have farming experience, in order to keep their families together, they agreed to move to the sugar beet fields around Lethbridge. Such a move meant that fathers and older brothers would not have to go to road camps. The farmers preferred older, able-bodied men and did not really want families with young children. The journey was made by train to Calgary, then to Lethbridge, where the people were dispersed to farmers in the surrounding area. They traveled in a coach attached to the end of a freight train, forced to sleep sitting up, during the days-long journey. The coaches were crowded and people were frightened and upset, not knowing what awaited them.

Despite promises of housing, once the Japanese arrived on the farms in southern Alberta, they often found themselves faced with inadequate living conditions. Previous beet workers had largely been single, migratory labourers, who had lived in shacks on the farms, but only during the beet season, and moved to cities for the cold winter months. Some of the farmers came to realize that the shacks had to be improved with tarpaper, felt paper, and wooden boards, to make them livable for families with small children. Water, for drinking and washing, had to be collected from rainfall, or hauled from distant wells. Many of the evacuees did not earn enough in the summer and fall of 1942 to survive the first winter. The families only became self-supporting once arrangements were made for males to work in lumber camps during the winter. Other evacuees were allowed to work in canning factories, such as the Broder Canning Company in Lethbridge, but only on the condition that they return to the farms after the end of the canning season.

The total number of Japanese brought into southern Alberta from B.C. was about 2,250 or about 370 families. By

1945, the evacuees constituted 65 percent of the beet labour in southern Alberta and were therefore considered an almost indispensable workforce in the province. However, under wartime regulations, they had no right of free movement, no right to buy or lease land, and were prevented from voting in the August 1944 provincial elections on the grounds that they were "temporary residents only."

In fact, most of the farmers looked upon the evacuees as a ready source of labour, and easily exploited. Probably no other group of evacuees had to suffer as much harrowing deprivation and hardship, working the long hours of tedious, backbreaking labour in the sugar beet fields. Working the sugar beets entailed thinning the plants in the spring, hoeing weeds and irrigating the fields during the growing season, and the really hard work of harvesting the sugar beets, which was done as late as November, or even December. For those who had once owned their own farms, boats and businesses, it must have been humiliating to be reduced to doing menial labour in strange surroundings.

By harvest time, the sugar beets had grown to the size of pineapples. Once they were ploughed up and loosened, they had to be pulled up out of the ground by hand, and the tops cut off, through the use of a machete-like implement with a C-shaped hook on the end. It took skill and practice to quickly and efficiently chop off the leaves, with one or two swift movements. Then the topped beets were thrown into a truck box behind them, or kicked into a line, so that a motorized pick-up implement could transfer them onto a passing truck. The workers were not used to such hard labour, even though they had been fishermen, farmers, or loggers in B.C. In addition, the pay was hardly enough to buy groceries for the families, and contrary to previous government promises, there were no welfare programs and no unemployment benefits. At first, most families could not afford to send their younger members to school, which cost seven dollars a month for each child to go to high school in Alberta. Any money that had been in savings had had to be used for winter clothes and boots, items that the families had never needed for the milder climate in B.C.

The cities remained out of bounds to the Japanese. Most of Alberta's city councils—including Lethbridge, Edmonton, and Calgary—had passed local ordinances, which prohibited Japanese from moving within their city limits. When any of the councils received a request for a Japanese Canadian to move into town—whether the person were originally from British Columbia or Alberta—it would cause an uproar in the council chambers. The requests were rejected, whether made by a prospective employer, a prospective employee or student. The fact of the person's ethnicity was sufficient reason for the refusal of the request.

According to some sources, the City of Lethbridge had a by-law in force, restricting Japanese Canadians from residing within the city limits, and it was only repealed in 1951. Lethbridge soon became known as an "anti-Japanese" city, after its city council not only banned *Nisei* girls who had obtained work as domestics, but also led a move to ban all Japanese from beer parlours and liquor outlets in the province. (It is quite a wonder, therefore, that barely 20 years later, the *Nikka Yuko* Japanese Garden—signifying friendship between Japan and Canada--was established as a Canadian centennial project in Lethbridge).

In contrast, the 1,000 evacuees who moved to the Manitoba beet fields encountered few problems of that kind. The largest proportion of evacuees seeking resettlement, however, moved to Ontario. Racial prejudice was spread over the whole of Canada, with a great deal of the anti-evacuee hostility radiating from municipal councils in eastern Canada.

However, the evacuees were not without help from many individuals who had become interested in their plight.

Church and YMCA groups, in particular, helped evacuees to find jobs and lodgings, and assisted *Nisei* social and political organizations, by offering free use of facilities.

Nakagama family's evacuation experience

"On May 24, 1942, Ryutaro and Nobuko Nakagama, along with their daughter, and their neighbours-- the Niwatsukino family--were the last remaining families to leave Steveston.

"My parents had responded to the government offer for a family of five to work together on a sugar beet farm in Alberta. In order to keep their family together, my parents, along with Aunt Miye, and her husband, Uncle Chosaburo, plus two male relatives, offered themselves as a unit of farm workers. The latter four went ahead to a farm near Picture Butte, while my parents and Rita followed later.

"The couple was relieved that an offer was received for rental of their store and residence during their absence. They were hopeful, therefore, that their property would be looked after, while they were gone. The store was rented by non-Japanese, and was the only store not boarded up by authorities. Since the family was given permission to remain a month longer to finalize the business and clean up their residence, they had more time to plan and pack. Furniture, non-essential clothing and household items were placed in storage. There were rumours in the community that the war couldn't last that long, and that people would probably be back in their homes within three months or so. As a result, for dishware, they packed only three rice bowls and six plates. In addition to basic household items and clothing, they decided to bring a sack of rice, personal valuables, photo albums, Japanese *kimono*, a sewing machine, and baby buggy. They felt more fortunate than families who had had to evacuate on short notice. Also, being on the last train, with fewer passengers and more space available on the freight car, they were given permission to bring more items than most other families.

"When their train arrived in Alberta, Japanese Canadians were not allowed to get off the train at a Calgary stop, nor at Lethbridge, until they were met by their future employers, the farm owners. For the Nakagama group, however, their farm owners were unable to meet them as new arrivals in Lethbridge, due to inclement weather that had made the farm roads temporarily impassable. The passengers were therefore required to stay on board for an additional three days. The food packed for the expected three-day trip had been eaten, but no one was allowed to leave the train to purchase any more. Fortunately, a Japanese person who had learned of their situation brought some food aboard for the passengers. He was a resident of Hardieville prior to the start of the war, who was working at a nearby restaurant in Lethbridge."

Nakagama family's early farm experiences: Coming to southern Alberta

"In May of 1942, the Nakagama family came to the Barron farm in Picture Butte, Alberta, and had to start working in the beet fields right away, by thinning the beet crop that was already growing. They had about 15 acres to work. The work was difficult and challenging, since the family members really had no experience with farming. In fact, for my city-bred mother, this was the first time she had ever even seen a hoe, much less have to use one.

"The family obtained a small payment from Mr. Barron after the thinning job was done, but this was the only money they received until harvest time, when they were given the bulk of their money for their beet work, based on every ton of beets produced. However, since the farm was small, they did not get a lot of money from the 15 acres. It was not adequate to support the number of workers in their group, so they only stayed at this farm for one year. During that first summer, they had to rely on money they had brought with them, just to make food purchases. The two males left after the first beet harvest, to work at a lumber camp in B.C. The five-member Nakagama family (my parents and older sister, still a young child, along with Aunt Miye and Uncle Chosaburo) moved on to a farm near Iron Springs that was more suited to their needs."

Living in a sugar beet shack

"The first shack that they had to use for accommodation had no insulation against severe winter weather. My mother has told us how snow blew in through the cracks in the walls in the wintertime, and weeds and wild grain grew through the floorboards in summer. The group of seven people had only three rooms -- a kitchen and two small bedrooms. My parents used one bedroom for themselves and Rita, and the other bedroom was divided into two, for the two male relatives and my aunt and uncle. Later, the family applied to the B.C. Security Commission, to make a few improvements to their quarters. They were able to add a third room, using materials received in the form of tarpaper and wood.

"The kitchen had a coal burning stove, a sink and a kitchen table. The beds were simple--wooden frames, with a mattress on wooden slats. Fortunately, the Barrons supplied the coal for fuel, and therefore the only expense incurred was for food. There were no utilities to pay, or any other kind of expenses for their meager lodging.

"My father did have enough money with him to buy an old car, when they first got to the Barron farm. They considered this a necessity, since they knew absolutely no one in the immediate area but had very close friends from Steveston (the Niwatsukino and the Sameshima families) now living near Turin. On some evenings, when they had time, and on the weekends, they would go for visits and picnics. This was their only form of socialization outside the farm during that first summer. In those days, it took about an hour to get to Turin, a distance of approximately 30 miles away.

"Although they had got a little bit of tarpaper, to block some of the cracks in the walls of the shack, in the winter the shack was bitterly cold. On cold winter evenings, it was often too cold to get into bed, so the group huddled around the coal burning stove with the doors of the stove open, sitting in front of it as long as possible. On some nights they would only get four or five hours of sleep. They really had very little to do on these evenings when their attention was centred on keeping warm around the stove. Ryutaro would sometimes read books that he had brought with him, and he would play some 'Solitaire' with playing cards. Rita recalls his deck of cards looking 'dog-eared,' but he was strongly opposed to idle card playing, when there were more productive things to be done."

Isolation

"Even in later years, my father was not fluent in English, but he was very interested in world events. Sometimes, he would take a copy of the newspaper and his Japanese/English dictionary into his office to attempt to read the news. Family members wonder whether this desire developed during the evacuation era, when they lived on the farm in Picture Butte. On the farm they had no electricity, as well as no access to radio, telephone or Japanese newspapers. Radios had been confiscated from them in Steveston and publication of the Japanese newspaper was stopped. Also, being new to the area, the family did not know the other Japanese families that had been evacuated to the same area, and so they lived in virtual isolation."

"The Nakagama family, including Aunt Miye, with members of the Niwatsukino family, Toshiko, Yoshiko, Tomiko, and Kazuko, on a Sunday picnic on the Alberta prairies, circa 1943. The two families were the last remaining in Steveston to be evacuated to the sugar beet farms in southern Alberta.

Hardships

"The most difficult challenge for the family at the Barron farm was obtaining water. The distance was the equivalent of almost a two-block walk from the shack to the well. The well was, of course, near the Barron farmhouse. The well water was the only potable supply, and they had to carry water back to the shack with two buckets attached to a pole, straddled over their shoulders. There was also a dugout or pond for the cows to drink, but this was also near the farmhouse, so the walking distance was the same. They had to use the well water only for drinking and cooking, but later on, the family was able to collect enough scrap lumber to build a bathhouse beside the dugout and use that water for their baths.

"The precious well water was first set aside for drinking and the rest used for food preparation. Definite planning went into the use of each drop of water. First, the rice was washed, with any leftover water used for washing other foods. The leftover water was then used to wash the dishes, and then it was used for laundry, and then finally used again to wash the floor or for any other general cleaning. All members of the household shared the job of toting water, since it was such hard work. In the winter, although they did not walk as far, the process was just as difficult, since they gathered snow from around the shack and melted it for their use. They even gathered up and melted the snow that had blown in from the cracks in the walls of the shack.

"My mother believes that the Japanese evacuees all had similar stories. Some had situations that were a little easier, while other situations made it more difficult. For example, if the family only had young children, it was more difficult. If a family had farm experience, they were more efficient in the fields and earned a little more money. Others had older males who could get hired out to other farms or do odd jobs, once they had finished with the chores at their assigned farm. My father was able to earn a little extra money by working for a friend near Picture Butte who was an accomplished carpenter. He did some odd jobs during the following summer. The Japanese did what they could, and what they had to do, to earn an honest living, whenever there was an opportunity to earn a little extra money."

Staying healthy

"Ryutaro's *judo* experience was helpful one day when Rita dislocated her shoulder when she was about four years old. He was able to work her shoulder back into place and he attributed this to his *judo* training and elementary knowledge of the anatomy. Going to the doctor was not routine then, as it is now, when doctors are close by. While growing up, the family members seldom went to the doctor, as my parents used Japanese holistic medicine to help cure minor ailments. For example, a simple cold or flu was treated with hot mustard plasters and/or hot towel compresses, various Japanese medicines--if they were available--enemas, and ice bags for aches and pains. My mother usually prepared Japanese dishes that she believed would help cure or ease their ailments, such as: *okayu* (soft-boiled rice) which is easily digestible; Japanese dishes such as *miso* (bean paste) soup; *tofu* (bean curd); etc. My father used Japanese methods such as *yaito*,[1] which was the basis for good massage techniques that he had acquired from his *judo* training and reading. He also used a machine called *noichi-shiki denki-anma* (electric current therapy), mainly used for muscle and joint pains.

"One time many years later, when my sister had to go to physiotherapy for tendonitis in her shoulder, the physiotherapist used a very similar machine on her, for treatment of her condition. My father studied--and became quite proficient—at applying chiropractic and massage techniques on his family members as well. Throughout the years,

---

1 *Yaito* was the use of "*Mogusa* powder," a pungent herb placed on a strategic acupressure point and burnt to stimulate that point.

many of them benefited from these treatments. My parents were always supportive of everyone in the family, or friends who had been injured or became ill, with even a simple flu. They would drop by their home to offer their assistance and make sure that the person was all right, and quite often my mother would bring along some type of Japanese dish she had prepared for the sick or injured person."

"The Nakagama family in 1944, with Rita and Sue (ages 5 and 1, respectively), taken on the occasion of a wedding of close family friends."

Setting up business in Alberta

"By 1946, realizing that all of their former life in Steveston was lost, and disliking farm work, my father decided to again try business, this time in Alberta. He began by purchasing an old truck and started a peddling/delivery business of fresh fish, obtained from an outlet in Shaughnessy, AB. He provided service to Japanese families working on area farms. Most of them were impoverished due to the evacuation, and with no mode of transportation, but with a hunger for traditional Japanese foods. Fish was the only product carried at this time, as rice and basic staple foods were available from the *Kobai-bu*, a co-operative enterprise set up by the local Buddhist Church for its members.

"My father had tremendous respect for farmers, as he saw them as extremely hard workers, and he would threaten to send us kids 'to the farm', whenever we misbehaved. He thought that as city kids we 'had it too good'. However, the behavioural standards that he and my mother demanded of us, as children, were as high as those they held for themselves.

"In the early years, when my father did his *sho-bai* business, peddling his goods to the rural areas, he happened to come to a farm where he found a young boy in the irrigation ditch, and saved him from drowning. He was the youngest family member, and only a toddler at the time, and had been left sleeping in the family car, while the rest of his family went to work in the nearby fields, but he had somehow managed to get out of the car. Ironically, when he grew up, the young boy became one of my father's sons-in-law.

"In the summer of 1946, with the help of friends as interpreters--Mr. Gochan Uyeda, Mr. Shouamon Yamada, and others—my father applied to the City of Lethbridge, to open and operate a Japanese grocery/rice/fish store on rented premises at 1st Avenue South. The main argument in his submission was that there were over 3,000 Japanese people scattered around, on farms in southern Alberta, and therefore, a central store to supply Japanese-type foods and staples was needed. The population east of Lethbridge, in small towns, had little or no access to these foods. The initial application was denied. My father applied and re-applied, even though it was generally known at the time that no Japanese evacuees were allowed to live in the city. There were persons performing domestic or other day work in the city, but they were all required to leave the city at night and on weekends. People believed that there were nightly 'curfew restrictions,' and that Japanese were discouraged from living in the city. However, my father persevered, and over the period of about a year, after several submissions and petitions, he obtained a special dispensation to set up his store within the city limits.

"The license to set up my father's business in Lethbridge was granted in the fall of 1947. The family moved into the city on October 15, 1947, when he set up the first Japanese food store and fish market in Alberta, located at 312 - 1st Avenue South, in Lethbridge. By this time, my parents had had three more daughters: Yoshiko (Sue), nearly four years old; Kimiko (Carol), one year old; and Mariko (Mary), barely a week old. With his family accompanying him, to live in the back of the store,

the Nakagama family became one of the first families who were Japanese Canadian evacuees to live
independently in Lethbridge. (I was the youngest
child, and only son, Kimio 'Kenny,' who joined the
family in 1954)."

(next page)

*"Trade and Business document for the Provincial Bureau of Statistics for
1949. Ryutaro was fortunate to have friends fluent in English-- such as
Mr. Seiji Omae, who filled in this particular form--when Ryutaro needed
help in completing documents and correspondence."*

CONFIDENTIAL

Form 1 L. S&s.

TO BE RETAINED BY YOUR OFFICE

GOVERNMENT OF THE PROVINCE OF ALBERTA
DEPARTMENT OF INDUSTRIES AND LABOUR
PROVINCIAL BUREAU OF STATISTICS

TRADES AND BUSINESSES, 1949

Being combined Statistics for the following:

Automotive Businesses and Garages, Barber Shops, Dyeing, Cleaning and Laundry Establishments, Hotels, Restaurants, Tailors, Retail and Wholesale Trades, etc.

P.S. If you did not operate the business for the entire year 1949, then please state the name and address of the former owner and/or the name and address of the person to whom you sold the business.

Issued jointly by the Provincial Bureau of Statistics and the Board of Industrial Relations, being a return required in accordance with the provisions of the following Acts:

"The Department of Industries and Labour Act, Chapter 14 of The Revised Statutes of Alberta, 1942. and amendments thereto."

"The Alberta Labour Act, Chapter 8, of the Statutes of Alberta, 1947, and amendments thereto."

and is directed _Groceries /Japanese Fish Mdse. Confectionery_ Trade or Business.
(State the name of main trade or business suspect to be got established.)

Reports should be submitted concerning the Trade or Business for which Provincial License has been obtained.

TRADE NAME _Nacagama Fish Nagget_

ADDRESS _362-1st Bt. S. Lethbridge—alta_

ESTABLISHMENTS, PLANTS OR UNITS .... No. ....

Location ....

Location ....

Location ....

N.B.—Where a firm has a branch or branches of the business .... at other points, it will be necessary to furnish a separate report for ....

---

6. **LIABILITIES:** State liabilities as at December 31st,1949, (omit cents).

Trade or Business	Bills Payable	Accounts Payable	Other Liabilities	Total Liabilities
	$	$	$	$
Automotive Business and Garage				
Barber Shops				
Dyeing, Cleaning and Laundry				
Hotels				
Restaurants				
Tailors				
Retail Trade				
Wholesale Trade				
(Other (specify)				
TOTAL	$	$	$	$

7. **GROSS SALES OR RECEIPTS:** State the aggregate dollars of Gross Sales or Receipts for the twelve months ended December 31st, 1949. $ .... (Gross Sout or Receipts in Dollars)

(a) **DISTRIBUTION OF GROSS SALES OR RECEIPTS** (omit cents) by classifications of Trade or Business:

Trade or Business	Amount		Trade or Business	Amount
By—	$		By—	$
Automotive Business and Garage			Wholesale Trade	
Barber Shops			Other (specify)	
Dyeing, Cleaning and Laundry				
Hotels				
Restaurants				
Tailors				
Retail Trade				
			GRAND TOTAL	$

(b) **DISTRIBUTION OF GROSS SALES OR RECEIPTS** (omit cents) by BRANCH ESTABLISHMENTS or Locations:

Branch Establishments or Locations	Automotive Businesses and Garage	Barber Shops	Dyeing, Cleaning and Laundry	Hotels	Restaurants	Tailors	Retail Trade	Whole-sale Trade	Other (specify)	TOTAL
	$	$	$	$	$	$	$	$	$	$

114908

The store

"The building was originally a restaurant, with rental rooms on the second floor. Behind the main building was a smaller one, split into two large one-room units. The main floor contained converted store space, a long narrow room adjacent to the store space used for private quarters, and a restaurant-style kitchen in the back, which had a walk-in cooler. Since there were no freezers in their first building, in order to store the fish, my father used an ice container placed inside the walk-in cooler, and additionally purchased blocks of ice to pack around the fish, to keep them fresh. (When he built the second store on 2nd Avenue, a similar style walk-in cooler was built, and from that period on, freezers were added, as needed, around the building to the total of six in use today.)"

"Ryutaro's first truck that he used to make his rounds visiting the rural customers in southern Alberta. This personalized service was one of his basic strategic pillars for developing his business in pre-war Steveston, and then again in post-war southern Alberta."

"Original inventory consisted mainly of staples – rice, tea, *shoyu, miso,* fish, and a few canned goods. With the large store space and insufficient capital to fully stock the shelves, he initially filled empty spaces with rolls of toilet paper. With few other Japanese families resident in the city, and most on the farms still without transportation, my father continued with a peddling/delivery service to rural areas, carrying fresh fish and groceries from the store. The fish was stored in a metal container in the back of the truck, and packed in ice, which he was able to replenish at towns along the way, as needed. On his return to the store in Lethbridge, he would dump the melted ice in the back alley.

"My mother looked after the store and the children in his absences, and also took in seamstress work, to supplement the family income. The family lived on the same premises adjacent to the store space on the main floor in the first store, and in later years at the second building, they lived behind the store, which was built with living quarters in the back. (The rooms upstairs in both buildings were always all rental units, although as my sisters grew older, the rooms were sometimes used by them as separate bedrooms for themselves.)"

Room rental—"a port in a storm"

"Over the years—from approximately 1948 to present—my father rented rooms in his store building, mostly to single men who worked in the city. It gave them a comfortable home base, where language and customs were familiar. Young Japanese people, who needed a place to stay during the week, started to come into the city by bus, to either find work or further their education. The rooms above the first store became rental units, since the original owners had left single beds in each room, with blankets and pillows. Unable to afford sheets, however, my mother bleached rice sacks and sewed them together for bed linens. She had to hand-wash them, until a wringer washer could eventually be purchased. At times, rentals involved up to six rooms upstairs, mainly to single persons, with two units in the back rented to couples. The Nakagama family of six used the room adjacent to the store, for sleeping quarters, with three beds stacked together. A small desk in one corner served as the store 'office'."

"One hand-sink and one toilet on the second floor of the main building served both the family and the renters. The family used a washtub for bathing, with an old rain barrel rigged up as a Japanese style 'soaking tub' in the kitchen, which was a weekly ritual. There was no central heating; a stove in the store and another in a central area upstairs, provided heating. There was also a cooking area for the tenants. Although a welcome 'port in the storm' for Japanese Canadians, it was somewhat of a dismal start for young persons first entering the city."

Serving the farm community

"Gradually, Japanese families started to move into the City of Lethbridge, but as the majority still resided on farms, my father continued traveling to rural areas for about 15 years, four days a week. Taber district was the farthest, taking two days to cover, as farms were scattered and road conditions poor. He used an old vehicle (the trip from

Lethbridge to Taber at that time took about two hours), sometimes sleeping overnight in the truck to complete the route. He always commented on the warm reception he received from the rural customers and he strove to give extra service, whenever he could. He extended credit when a family needed it, and he would often try to have some candy or treats for the children on the various farms he visited."

Store products

"A few food wholesalers--such as Nishizawa Company and Amano Company--with whom business relationships had been established in pre-war Steveston, had resumed business in post-war Vancouver. They became the primary suppliers for the Alberta business. As finances improved, my father continually searched for new and quality Japanese food products and rice for his customers. In this effort, he tried direct import from Japan for a time, but found it not economically feasible, due to small volume shipping. Fish was supplied by Lions Gate Fisheries. Though Nishizawa Co. has since ceased operation, Amano and Lions Gate continue as suppliers today.

"Wanting to add fresh foods to his product line, my father started experimenting with a food specialty remembered from his native Kagoshima, *kamaboko* and *satsuma-age* (both are varieties of fish cakes). A table-ready food, production required the deboned flesh of the fish to be broken down, mixed into a batter and shaped into small cakes, for steam cooking or deep-frying. Lacking proper equipment, he carved mallets from tree branches, and together with my mother, tried pounding and mixing the raw fish into a batter in a wooden *shoyu* keg, placed on the floor. After several attempts and failures, they developed a recipe and a saleable product. As it became popular with the Japanese customers, the need for automated equipment to streamline the process became a priority. My father consulted with Mr. Sam Kosaka, who was in the welding business, to develop the automated grinder, mixer, and equipment and tools still in use today. Though the fish batter still required manual shaping into individual cakes, the new equipment eased the heavier work involved. In time, a few cottage-type businesses in the area also supplied fresh items, such as *tofu*, *udon* and *chow mein* noodles. When fresh *tofu* became unavailable, he experimented with, and made his own supply, in-store. Bean sprouts, grown in the basement, were also tried for a short time."

"Ryutaro and Nobuko Nakagama making tofu in the kitchen of the second store (circa 1980). The value-added work of making tofu, fish cakes, sushi, etc., was another important pillar to the development of the store's varied product lines."

"One of the grandchildren has fond memories of watching her grandfather spend hours making *kamaboko* (steamed fish cake), attempting to perfect each one to be identical to the next, as he smoothed the batter onto each steel plate.[2] I remember my father cooking small, bite-size pieces

2 Originally, *kamaboko* was formed by hand into a slab, onto flat pieces of wood, and sold with the wooden plate attached. But Ryutaro came up with the idea of using metal plates so that the *kamaboko*, once steam-cooked, could then be sliced off the metal plates and they could then be reused.

of *satsuma-age* (deep fried fish cake) as a treat to give to the dog. He loved animals so much. He had a real look of joy on his face when he tossed the ball around for the dog, but his greatest love was for cats. Before he married, my father had owned a black cat, but he was saddened when it left one day and never returned. My mother asked him once why he had had a cat, and his reply was that whenever he had felt worried, troubled or lonely, stroking his cat had greatly comforted him."

Introduction of Japanese-style rice to the Japanese Canadian market

"Although rice was a staple food for the Japanese, long-grain rice (Chinese style) was the only rice available locally, at the time. Therefore, a primary objective throughout the early years was to find quality short-grain rice, which was more suited to the Japanese palate. He had heard (or read) about short-grain rice grown in California. With no known supplier or contact, my father wrote an enquiry on speculation, enclosing a few dollars, to a Japanese hotel he had heard about, possibly the Kusano Hotel in San Francisco. Though he held little expectation for results, he thought there might be some connection, and in due time, a reply was received, with a referral to Nomura and Company, which marketed Kokuho Calrose Rice, produced by Koda Brothers Company. My father constantly expressed gratitude for the sincerity and kindness of the hotel manager, for following-up on the enquiry of an unknown party from Canada! Though he had a few concerns, and no personal knowledge of the actual product, he decided to pursue the recommendation and take the financial risk of importing a sufficient quantity of the rice to begin marketing it in Canada. This became a pivotal turning point for the future of his business. The producers later developed Kokuho Rose rice, an international award winner, considered one of the highest quality types of short-grain rice in the United States. With the Kokuho rice, my father had found a product that better suited the majority of the Japanese population, and that had not been available in Canada until then.

"After commencing negotiations with the company, and after months of dealing with issues of importation, customs, establishing credit, financing, and arranging transportation, Kokuho rice was first introduced into Canada at his Lethbridge store. I often wondered how he was able to meet all the complex requirements of importation, but have since learned that with the help of good friends, such as Mr. Seiji Omae, he was able to provide the necessary English correspondence and documents. Later, family members would assist my father in English-letter writing for claims and inquiries."

In retrospect

"My father believed that starting a new life and business in Alberta had been the right decision for him. Similar to all the evacuees to Alberta, my father and mother endured great hardship, but characteristic of the Japanese Canadians as a whole, I am struck with how they turned adversity into opportunity. They focused on getting through each day, hoping for a better life, and seemed to never allow their dream to be stolen from them. I am most impressed by the fact that, despite having lost so much in Steveston, they never became bitter, as they established a new home in southern Alberta. Whenever I asked him about coming to Alberta, he emphasized how much he believed that starting a new life and business here was the right decision."

CHAPTER 12

Post-war Developments

Anti-Japanese hostility east of the Rockies generally abated after the end of the war, although wartime controls on the Japanese were not lifted until March 31, 1949. On that date, the Japanese were finally free to vote in federal elections anywhere in Canada and were free to move anywhere in Canada, even back into the 100-mile protected area along the west coast. For most, however, it was not a matter of "going home," or resuming former occupations and positions, because their homes, businesses, farms and boats had been confiscated and sold.

After a three-year debate between citizen and civic groups of Alberta with the Alberta government—based on material and moral grounds--in March of 1948, Premier Ernest Manning announced that Japanese Canadian residents of Alberta were entitled to the same rights and privileges as any other Albertan. Nevertheless, Japanese Canadians still faced discrimination in the workplace, in housing and in education.

Of the approximately 2,500 Japanese who were sent to Alberta as sugar beet labourers, a group of them formed the Japanese Canadian Citizens' Association, consisting of delegates from the surrounding districts of southern Alberta. They became part of the National Association of Japanese Canadians, with headquarters in Toronto. The local organization was active in petitioning for abolition of restrictions against immigration of "strandees" (people born in Canada, but stranded in Japan during the war.) They helped, and gave moral support to, the Potato Growers' Association because of difficulties experienced by potato growers in the two consecutive years of 1950 and 1951. They were also involved in political issues. On February 15, 1952, at a provincial JCCA council meeting, Ted Aoki reported submission of a brief to the Lethbridge local Alberta Teachers' Association, asking for endorsement for the withdrawal of a textbook that was being used as a high school reference manual. The reason was the prevalent use of the word "Jap." As a result of his efforts, the book was revised.

From the year 1955 to 1977, the Japanese Canadian Citizens' Association was dormant until the Centennial year, 1977, when there was a resurgence of interest, both nationally and locally, as programs were planned for celebrating the 100 years since Manzo Nagano had entered Canada. The organization sponsored many activities and events over the years, including the *keiro-kai* (seniors' parties) and obtaining the redress for all of the eligible Japanese Canadians in southern Alberta.

Local members of the LDJCA were involved in the national Redress movement, which took place over a period of eight years or so. Two members worked particularly hard, attending meetings in Toronto, Montreal, Ottawa, Vancouver, or Winnipeg, on their own time, and often at their own expense. Their dedicated efforts, along with those of a local committee of eight members, culminated in an announcement on September 22, 1988 of a public apology by the Canadian government, along with a monetary compensation to surviving individuals of Japanese Canadian descent born prior to March 31, 1949. A lump sum was also given to the National Organization to administer and allocate among its member chapters, groups, and individuals, for arts, sports, and cultural projects and events.

In 2001, the LDJCA published a history book, entitled, *Nishiki: Nikkei Tapestry, a History of Southern Alberta Japanese Canadians.* It contained stories about Japanese Canadian businesses, organizations, and individuals, as well as family stories. Later that year, the LDJCA officially dissolved in favour of an umbrella organization, the Nikkei Cultural Society of Lethbridge and Area, to promote an awareness and appreciation of Japanese culture in the community, and to coordinate various Japanese Canadian organizations and activities, with representatives from church groups, the new immigrants, and various community and sports organizations.

Business accomplishments of the mid-years

"In the fall of 1950, when the first truckload of 220 sacks (22,000 lbs.) of Kokuho brand rice arrived in Lethbridge, it was an instant success with the Japanese community. Storage space was rented in an adjacent building, and for many years, my father single-handedly unloaded the 100-lb. sacks into the storage area and storefront, as shipments arrived several times a year. Eventually, these shipments grew to 80,000 lbs. each, shipped by rail car, and help had to be hired for the unloading process.

"In appreciation from the producers who had been looking into the Canadian export market, the company granted my father the Canadian franchise and informal appointment as sole distributor of the rice in Canada at this time. This introduced

considerable future business dealings with whole-
salers and retailers, to promote Kokuho Rice across
Canada, e.g., Amano and Nishizawa in B.C.; Furuya
and Union in Toronto; and many others. With rice
being the basic staple of the Japanese diet, my father considered it as one of the proudest accomplishments and satisfactions of his business career:
the discovery and work expended in successfully
importing quality short-grain rice into Canada, and
its immediate popularity with the entire Japanese
community."

*"Ryutaro and Nobuko Nakagama behind the counter of the 2ⁿᵈ Avenue
store (circa 1960). Customers were originally served from behind this
counter, with items collected for them by the clerk."*

"By 1955, business had grown to a degree whereby, with the help of investing friends and relatives, he was able to purchase two city lots and build the current building at 322 – 2nd Avenue South. This new structure had a main floor store, living quarters in the back, and apartment suites on the second floor. With this move, he was able to expand the business, adding cookware, dishware, giftware, and novelties to the food inventory. By the early 1960s, delivery to rural areas was no longer necessary. Most families had vehicles and were independent and mobile, progressing to resemble today's modern consumer.

"Over the years, from the initial start with fresh fish, he then expanded into staples, such as rice, *shoyu, miso,* tea; and then fresh products such as: *satsuma-age, kamaboko, tofu, udon, chow mein, age;* canned and dried foods, such as *nori* and *konbu* (both are types of seaweed), noodles; frozen and instant foods; Japanese snack foods and candies. In later years, expanded inventory included rice cookers, utensils, dishware, giftware, dolls, books, subscription magazines, videotapes of programs from Japan, and Buddhist shrine items."

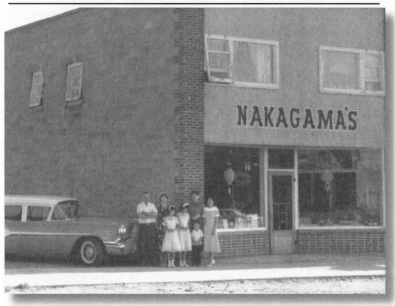

"The Nakagama family posing for a picture in front of their second store on 2ⁿᵈ Avenue in Lethbridge, AB (circa 1959)."

"My father rarely displayed much humour at home, as he was usually preoccupied with the store and business matters, but we learned from friends and customers that he had a great sense of humour outside the family circle. I was really surprised as a teenager, when some of my friends told me how much fun my father was at weddings and social gatherings. He loved to sing at weddings, particularly *shigin*,[3] and loved traditional Japanese dance. He once rewrote the lyrics to a popular Japanese song, *Nagasaki Ochosan* ('Madame Butterfly of Nagasaki'), which expressed the conditions and hardships of life in evacuation era Alberta. The image of the sugar beet woman as *Ochosan* (Madame Butterfly) had everybody roaring with laughter.

---

3 *Shigin* is a very old traditional form of poetry, which is presented in a song or chant, accompanied by a Japanese musical instrument.

"Occasionally, he enjoyed participating in the community *engai-kai*.[4] (He once even choreographed his own dance, which he presented in traditional dress on stage, using a *katana* or *samurai* sword). In later years, he became more playful with family members. When my brothers-in-law took me out to a bar to celebrate my 21st birthday—I was the youngest one in the family—my father was a good sport, and joined in the fun. Some of his grandsons remember Grandpa joining in with them when playing pool. They said that even though they couldn't really talk to him in English, it was 'quite neat.' My dad always tried to mix in with his grandchildren, with whatever they were doing."

Business details of the later years

"At the outset, customers were served from behind the counter, with all items being retrieved by the store workers. Later, renovations were made to facilitate self-service, with items to purchase being brought to the cash desk at the side of the store. However, my father continued to cut and package fish and other products, as required. There was also the 'value-added work,' consisting of the vacuum sealing of fresh foods, or foods purchased in bulk and repackaged in the store. With the increase in food preparation technology, there was also considerable expansion of food inventory to more instant-type food products.

"Over the years, customers have come from Alberta, interior B.C., southern Saskatchewan, northern Canada, Alaska, and Montana. Some are Japanese who married Canadians or Americans

---

4 *Engai-kai* were amateur variety and drama concerts organized by the Japanese evacuees, with songs and dances.

of other ethnic groups. Others have emigrated from Japan; many were sponsored to work on local Japanese farms. Recently, with educational and cultural exchanges, many customers are students from Asia, shopping for 'comfort' foods—a situation very similar to the service provided so many years ago for evacuees, far from their homeland of Japan, and their 'second home' on the west coast.

"Some customers may phone ahead for special products, otherwise there are no 'standing orders.' However, orders are taken for special occasions-- organizational and social functions, and during the year-end Christmas and New Year's rush--to ensure that fresh and specialty products are available from B.C. suppliers, and store-made products are sufficient to fill volume orders."

"Nobuko Nakagama, and son, Ken, behind counter at 2nd Avenue store, Lethbridge, AB (circa 1991). Customers were now serving themselves, from products on the shelves, and bringing them to the cash counter for checkout.

"Over the years, my father continued to provide personalized service, which was an important pillar for his business plan. He always tried to give a personalized touch towards the service of his customers, which I try to emulate to this day. There has also been a dramatic increase in requests for instructional assistance, recipes, etc. to give to members of the younger generation, grandchildren, and customers new to Japanese foods, inter-racial marriage partners, and those simply interested in trying new and different foods. In recent years, Japanese food has enjoyed an increase in interest and popularity, both for its novelty, and its healthfulness.

"Occasionally, *sushi* and Japanese food demonstrations, are requested by different organizations, and are provided, as time permits. Catering initially began in the early days with *sashimi* trays for weddings and different social functions. Although there are still occasional orders for *sashimi*, the majority of requests now are for *sushi* trays for weddings, meetings, and other social functions.

"As Japanese foods have gained in popularity in recent years, the Nakagama business has again been able to adapt, to ensure future growth and viability. *Sushi* is prepared each Friday and Saturday, and made up into 50 box lunches (*bento* boxes), each with seven pieces of *sushi*; all boxes are sold out every week. The standard weekly production is 25 *maki-sushi* (large rolls with various kinds of filling) and 60 *inari-sushi* ('rice bags'). My mother developed the recipe combinations for volume production, taught us the making and handling of rice and *sushi*, and provided input into production problems. She actually rolled the *sushi*, even as an octogenarian, and was still responsible for cooking and preparing the *gu* (inside filling for *sushi*) – *shitake* (Japanese mushroom), *kampyo* (dried gourd), egg, cucumber or spinach, ginger--and having them ready for the actual *sushi*-making function. Now in her 90s, she is still coming into the store four times a week, taking an active interest in overall production and quality control.

"The Nakagama store has been basically a family-run business, though in the mid-1950s and early 60s, when the children were young, help was received from live-in employees, to work in the kitchen and store. Numerous part-time and seasonal employees have been part of the operation over the years. Today, two clerks cover weekdays and two students work on weekends.

"Over the years, the store has served as something of a social centre for the Japanese community. Particularly in the early years, when customers would have a chance meeting at the store, there were greetings and visiting, as most had not seen each other for a long time. All of the staff at the store take a personal interest in their customers and make the effort to learn people's names, and give cheerful and helpful service.

"As older, established customers are lost through attrition, the store has had to evolve, in order to find new customers. My parents had an original customer target group that was totally Japanese, but with the tremendous increase in interest in Japanese foods, our customer target is now the whole population of Lethbridge and southern Alberta. In fact, the larger proportion of customers is now non-Japanese.

"Since the business has been family-run, and for most of its years, mainly by my father himself, the family as a unit has been unable to take extended holidays. One of my great memories, when we were young, was Dad taking the whole family to a movie after Christmas dinner. 'Ma and Pa Kettle' movies were our favourites. Sometimes, dad would roll with laughter in his seat, as he watched these slapstick comedy shows. The grandchildren, especially, could get Grandma and Grandpa giggling over silly things, and it was fun to see their good sense of humour.

"Due to the store hours, my parents had been only able to take a few day trips, when possible on Sundays or holidays. When the children were young and the family quite poor, my father managed, however, to arrange some family outings. Because he could not be absent from the store too long, we were only able to take day trips, such as to Waterton National Park, which was quite close to Lethbridge, about 70 miles. On many Sundays, we would go there for picnics. Our parents sat up front in the cab of the truck, while the children climbed into the back, to travel to Waterton for the day. We have many fond memories of picnic lunches made by our mother that always consisted of *onigiri* (Japanese rice balls) and other Japanese dishes, which we ate on the lakeshore."

"The Nakagama family at a picnic in Waterton, AB, on a warm Sunday afternoon (circa 1952). Extended holidays were impossible for Ryutaro and his family in the early years of post-war southern Alberta. Nearby Waterton National Park was a favourite destination for the day, when time permitted."

"In the summertime, we would go as a family to the local fair and grandstand shows. My father loved the big rides and even tried his skill at the midway games. He was, in these instances, really a 'kid at heart.' My father was a passionate man who worked hard and played hard. Somehow, he managed to keep the two in balance. On holidays, or even a day trip to Waterton, my father showed a different side of himself, as he could forget about work and enjoy the time away.

"Both of my parents especially loved going to the hot springs, as they believed in their thera-peutic value. On long weekend holidays, when they could leave the store for a couple of days, the family would go to Banff or Radium Hot Springs. Later, when my father found someone to look after the store, family members would take holidays to Ainsworth Hot Springs in B.C. The grandchildren found it amazing to see how long their grandfather could sit inside the hot spring pools, while most of them would just take a quick dip in the hot pool and leave.

"As family members became older, and one or the other was able to watch the store, my parents took trips that usually combined business (Vancouver and San Francisco) with personal, e.g., to Vancouver to visit suppliers, plus visit family in Richmond. In later years, the couple did take some local trips with one or another family member. Also, they did take a couple of trips to Japan, again combining business with holiday and family visits.

"Similar specialty stores in Lethbridge have been competitors at times, but for various reasons, such as retirement or other opportunities, all have ceased operation after a time, with the exception of Asian Market, which specializes in all kinds of foods from various countries in the Orient. Today, the R. Nakagama Co., as from its origin, continues to focus only on Japanese foods and goods in Lethbridge. Competition from other businesses has generally helped--rather than hindered--their operation, to continually make improvements to maintain market share and sustain value and efficiency consciousness."

Family business

"After my father suffered a heart attack, during the years of 1965 and 1966, he recovered to a state of good health. Despite his doctor's advice to reduce his workload, he had no one to rely on for the heavy work, and so he was soon back to his normal work routine. In 1977, as my father's youngest child and only son, I entered a partnership in the store after graduating from the University of Calgary, with a degree in Commerce. My preparation for running the business was 'hands-on,' as I had observed and worked with my father on a day-to-day basis in the store.

"I wanted to join the store right after I graduated from university, but my mother was strongly and very fervently against me doing so. Having endured the struggles of developing and maintaining a business--albeit under very unusual and 'hard time' circumstances--she just didn't want to see me having to work the kind of hours and devote the labour needed in a single-owner store like ours. Neither did she want to see me having to dedicate my life totally to it, like my father had. My father supported the idea of my taking over the business, and probably from a man's viewpoint, was proud to have his son carry on with the operation.

"With my business degree, there were other career paths that I had also considered, like pursuing an accounting designation, but at that time, I was tempted by the prospect of someday owning and running my own business, and therein lay the appeal. I entered the partnership on a trial basis, but finally took over, the reason the store has continued as 'Nakagama's' for over 60 years."

"Ryutaro Nakagama beside a stack of 'Kokuho Rose' rice (circa 1982)."

CHAPTER 13

Early Pioneers to Southern Alberta

$\mathbf{T}$here was a population of pioneers in southern Alberta, who had immigrated in 1910 to 1920, and homesteaded and made a community for itself, particularly in the Raymond area. For various reasons, the Japanese arriving in southern Alberta experienced less racial hostility than the Japanese settling in British Columbia during the same time period. Important factors were probably the severe labour shortage in Alberta, coupled with the relatively smaller numbers of Japanese, as well as other immigrants from ethnic groups besides British and northern European.

The largest and earliest permanent Japanese settlement in southern Alberta was around Raymond, a farming town populated mostly by Mormons, who had arrived from the United States, themselves trying to escape persecution. About 20 Japanese men came in 1903 to work at the Raymond sugar factory. A wealthy Mormon industrialist from Utah had begun operating the Knight Sugar Factory in 1903, and had a desperate need for sugar beet workers. Then in 1908, about 100 Japanese came to Raymond through the efforts of a Japanese businessman who contracted rail and farm workers. The men were housed in three large tents, suffering from the cold and heat, due to extremes in weather.

In 1909, some 105 Japanese men were brought in, to break land for the Knight Sugar Factory, contracting some 1500 acres. The Japanese, along with other immigrant groups, worked in various camps organized by the Knight Company, in and around Raymond. The sudden influx of Japanese in Raymond aroused some local controversy, but community leaders made the point that for economic reasons, the factory had a right to get workers from wherever it could.

From working on the Knight farms and ranches, the Japanese were able to gain valuable farming experience that provided a foundation for them to set up their own farms, once the sugar factory closed in 1914. A number of Japanese men decided to open more virgin land and try their hand at grain farming, on the dry lands of the Milk River Ridge, mainly growing wheat, oats and barley. By 1916, the farmers had built houses, were ready to settle down, and sent for "picture brides" from Japan. They started raising grain and hay, growing vegetables for their own use, and also supplementing their diet with meat from hogs and chickens. Many descendants of these early pioneer farmers still live in southern Alberta.

CHAPTER 14

Japanese Food and Customs

Maintaining culture through food preparation and enjoyment has been an integral part of the continuance of Japanese culture in southern Alberta. The most important time of the year for the Japanese is New Year's Day, which is celebrated along with most Canadians, on January 1st, at which time families get together to feast on traditional foods.

Traditional Japanese dishes require elaborate preparation, but most are made out of a few basic foods—rice, fish, soybeans, and seaweed. The most indispensable food and staple diet of the Japanese is rice, which is also the basic raw material of *miso* and vinegar. The generic Japanese term for a meal is *gohan,* or "rice."

In earlier times, rice was part of the people's religious faith, and was offered to the gods in thanksgiving after every harvest. Some of the *Issei* and *Nisei* people continue to place the first scoop of cooked rice from every meal onto the ancestral altar in the home, in respect to deceased relatives and ancestors. When serving rice, two scoops—even if the second one is only ritualistic—must be given to each person; giving only one scoop is reserved for presentation to deceased ancestors.

Sushi is the general term for rice dishes that are eaten by hand, or by the mouthful. The simplest, everyday form is *onigiri,* or "riceball," which is simply a handful of rice pressed together in the cupped hands. In its simplest form, the wet hands are sprinkled with salt and the rice ball formed, so that it has a layer of salt on the outside. A Japanese pickled plum *(ume-boshi)* may be inserted in the middle, or a sheet of dried seaweed *(nori)* wrapped around it.

There are several different kinds of *sushi,* made individually, in rolls, or little bags (resembling tiny gunny sacks) made from a deep-fried soy bean preparation (like *tofu,* or soybean cake), but all types use rice that is seasoned lightly with sweetened vinegar. They are often eaten with soy sauce or *wasabi,* Japanese horseradish that is grated to produce a pale green, pungent condiment.

Miso, a yellowish-brown paste, is made by fermenting steamed, salted soybeans, rice, wheat, or other grains. *Shoyu* or soy sauce, was introduced to Japan from China, and is a basic element in almost all Japanese dishes. Along with *miso,* soy sauce is an indispensable flavoring element in Japanese cooking, not considered merely flavoring, but an essential part of life.

Sashimi, or raw seafood is a typical food of Japan, which is becoming well-known in Western cultures. Seafoods that are eaten raw—fish or shellfish—are eaten separately, or as part of sushi. Tuna, carp, mackerel, salmon, prawns, abalone, and mussels, are examples.

Different kinds of noodle dishes are commonly eaten for traditional meals or as everyday fare. *Soba* is a long, thin, brownish noodle made from buckwheat flour. It is traditionally eaten on New Year's Eve because the long thin noodles symbolize longevity. *Udon* is a noodle that is thicker than *soba,* and is whitish in colour, being made from kneaded wheat flour. Noodles can be served with different kinds of broth, and might be eaten hot or cold. In Japan, it is considered acceptable to make a slurping sound when eating noodles.

The daily diet in Japan uses rice as the staple, and includes vegetables and boiled, fried or roasted fish or meat, as well as *miso* soup and pickled vegetables. In preparing food in Japan, an ancient practice has been to avoid waste. For example, in the utilization of fish, the meat is used for *sashimi,* or eaten grilled or boiled, and other parts of the fish would be used for soup. Preserved foods have long been used to make up for shortages in lean years. Preservation methods include pickling for vegetables, and salting or drying, for fish and meat. Food is generally eaten using chopsticks, which are nearly always made of wood, and shaped from a pointed end to a thicker end. An ancient practice is to use the pointed end for eating, and using the larger end for serving oneself from the serving platter, as compared to the Chinese, for example, who traditionally use longer, thicker chopsticks that allow them to all eat from a communal serving bowl.

Breakfast is a plain and simple meal, lunch is fairly light, with the main emphasis put on the evening meal.

A most important principle of Japanese cooking, however, is the presentation: "First you eat with the eye."

CHAPTER 15

Cultural Integration

The early Japanese settlers in the Raymond area welcomed and supported the evacuees. The two groups slowly integrated over the years, to form a fairly cohesive group in southern Alberta, along with the third major group of Japanese immigrants, which again came to supply sugar beet workers in the 1970s. In an agreement between the Canadian and Japanese governments, agricultural training programs were made available to Japanese young people between 1969 and 1976, when over 222 young agricultural students came to southern Alberta to work on potato and sugar beet farms. In 1977, the Southern Alberta New Japanese Immigrant Association was formed, to assist and welcome new immigrants into the community, but also to help each other become successful and independent in whatever their chosen field.

Over the years, Japanese Canadian organizations have been both political and social. However, over the past 10 to 20 years, there has been less interest in maintaining the cultural heritage. The people from the first generation, or *Issei*, have mostly passed on. Those of the second generation, or *Nisei*, have mostly "closed the chapter" on their past memories. Shamed and embarrassed by their treatment by the government, they have tried to fit in as good citizens in their new communities throughout southern Alberta. By the 1960s, most of the Japanese had risen into the middle class, and intermarriage was seen in the majority, rather than the minority, of marriages involving Japanese Canadians. The third generation, *Sansei,* however, has been more open to looking at the past, to question and examine historical events.

Sansei people have had the perspective of distance--as compared to the *Issei* and *Nisei*. This gives some objectivity, as well as the desire or ability to speak about the experience. The Japanese culture is shame-based, which means that children are raised to not embarrass their family, to not "stick out" from the rest of the Japanese Canadian community. The pioneers in the early 1900s, therefore, adapted to the life of the farming communities and were accepted by their peers. The Japanese also have a cultural motto which translates, "It can't be helped," which led to a quiet acceptance of the evacuation orders during World War II, and later, a reputation for hard work, perseverance, and dignity that led to a general community acceptance of Japanese Canadians in southern Alberta.

Japanese Canadians have achieved assimilation and acceptance into the Canadian culture mainly through an emphasis on education, the value of hard work, and law-abiding behaviour. As a result of these behaviours, many have come to call them a "model minority." Rather than succumbing to social and economic pressures, the Japanese people have probably become one of Canada's most resourceful and progressive minority groups. The evacuation and relocation broke up the ghettos of the west coast, but ironically, this process had the effect of pushing the Japanese Canadians headlong into a drive for cultural assimilation, displayed through the outward signs of middle-class status in society. While there have been few Japanese Canadians who have risen to levels of public or corporate power, prestige, or privilege, there is a phenomenon of persistence, resulting in admirable occupational and educational attainment among Japanese descendants.

Nakagama family's connections to Japanese culture

"The entire immediate family of Ryutaro and Nobuko Nakagama was closely tied to the Japanese culture and heritage, because of the constant exposure to cultural activities through the store. Being the principal residence, the store was an integral part of the lives of all family members over the years. Most of the meals for family gatherings featured Japanese foods cooked by my mother, with *sashimi* prepared by my father. Grandpa would remember who liked what foods and would offer the last remaining part of a dish to the person he knew loved it the most, but he still did his best to treat all his grandchildren equally and the same.

"For special occasions, many times the table was set up in the store front, amongst the Japanese groceries and sacks of rice, with the front windows covered over with paper for privacy! As a result, the children and grandchildren were all influenced by the culture and heritage, and took an active interest in their cultural and family history.

"One grandchild recollects that, 'Grandpa never raised his voice to us.' The story is told that when the grandchildren were quite young and they happened to be at the store after hours, he would let them run and play in the store. But sometimes, they would get into mischief and mix up the *moyashi mame* (green mung beans) with the *azuki* beans (red beans) that were displayed in open bins in the store: 'Grandpa sat us down and showed us how to separate the beans. We tried, but they were such small beans that our parents had to finish the job. I don't think we were the only kids who did this, but Grandpa never really got mad about it.'

"In the early years, my sisters were active in *odori* (Japanese dancing) at the various *engai-kai* (Japanese drama) gatherings organized by the evacuees around southern Alberta, as were my parents. Of their grandchildren, some wrote school papers about the Japanese Canadians and their own family histories. For example, one in post-secondary school wrote about the store for his thesis in working toward his business degree. Although none of my sisters took *judo*, I took up the sport, and six of eight grandchildren were involved in *judo* at various points in their lives. The youngest grandson, now in university, is still very active in the sport.

"As our father grew older, he more often showed another side of his personality. From time to time, the family glimpsed a softer, kinder person, but never as much as when the grandchildren were around. He loved to get on the floor and wrestle with his grandsons, showing them his many *judo* moves. His wish was to have all his grandchildren take up this sport, and he would have been proud to know that one of his grandsons obtained his black belt in *judo*. He didn't just favour the boys, either.

"One granddaughter remembers that even though she was a girl, Grandpa would turn her upside-down on the carpet too, and they would both laugh and laugh. It was amusing to see my father picking up one of his granddaughters, carrying her around the store with him, as he went about his work.

"One grandson spent four years in Japan on the Japan-English Teaching program and decided to pursue post-graduate studies in Asian/Japanese Studies, and one granddaughter also went to Japan on the same program, later furthering her studies in Culture and Sociology, both of them studying abroad.

"My parents were denied many things and they made many sacrifices. However, they had a significant influence on their children and grandchildren. I believe they opened up the path for the younger generation to be able to make the choices they can today. The connection to their culture, and the interest of the *Sansei/Yonsei* (third/fourth) generation in our heritage, is a testimony to the strong influence and teachings of my parents who paved the way. I believe that there are many similar examples in many of the Japanese Canadian families who have gained acceptance into society as a whole, while still maintaining many of their traditional cultural ways."

Ryutaro and Nobuko Nakagama, 50th wedding anniversary

CHAPTER 16

Traditional values

Traditional values were the basis of the Japanese Canadians' respect, compliance and resiliency: *enryo*—reserve, restraint; *gaman*—patience, perseverance; and *shikata-ga-nai* ("it can't be helped"). These provided a strong basis for them to ultimately survive the events of the evacuation. In addition, a basic cultural tenet of *on*—limitless devotion, obedience, or sense of indebtedness—must also be seen as being the foundation of Japanese Canadian behaviour that guided everyday behaviour, but was particularly evident when faced with evacuation orders. Children in Japan are taught this lesson very early, as evidenced by this little story from a Japanese second-grade school reader entitled, "Don't forget the *on*":

> Hachi is a cute dog. As soon as he was born he was taken away by a stranger and was loved like a child of the house. For that reason, even his weak body became healthy and when his master went to his work every morning, he would accompany him (master) to the streetcar station and in the evening around the time when he (master) came home, he

went again up to the station to meet him.

In due time, the master passed away. Hachi, whether he knew of this or not, kept looking for his master every day. Going to the usual station he would look to see if his master was in the crowd of people who came out whenever the streetcar arrived.

In this way days and months passed by. One year passed, two years passed, three years passed, even when ten years had passed, the aged Hachi's figure can be seen every day in front of the station, still looking for his master.

School children in Japan, and even *Nisei* in Canada, know this story. A monument to Hachi stands in a public place in Japan, to remind passers-by of their obligation to parents and their superiors. In Japanese culture, it is experienced as a heavy personal burden, always overriding one's personal preferences. It is not a story about pity, but about piety.

EPILOGUE

In 2009, a Hollywood movie was released, starring Richard Gere (whom I have heard is one-quarter Japanese), in which the story of Hachi is re-enacted, based on the original, but this time in an American setting. The movie is entitled, "Hachiko: A dog's story," depicting the loyalty of a dog—in this case, an Akita pup (Japanese breed) which had been sent from Japan. He got loose in an American train station, and was found and raised by a college professor. Hachi became a devoted companion, accompanying his master to the commuter train station in the morning, and then meeting him later in the day, when the professor returned from work on the five o'clock train. One day, the professor died suddenly while at work, but Hachi continued to keep up a daily vigil for his master for nine years, until he himself died.

In the movie, the dog's remarkable behaviour teaches the local people about undying love, unending compassion, but especially, unyielding loyalty. The original story and bronze statue of the original Hachiko are shown at the end of the movie.

BIBLIOGRAPHY

Adachi, K. (1976). *The enemy that never was: A history of the Japanese Canadians.* Toronto: McClelland & Stewart.

Aoki, R. (2005-2010). Personal communication.

Benedict, R. (1946). *The chrysanthemum and the sword: Patterns of Japanese culture.* Rutland, VT: Charles E. Tuttle.

Japan Travel Bureau. (1994). *A look into Japan.* Japan.

Lethbridge and District Japanese Canadian Association. (2001). *Nishiki, Nikkei tapestry, a history of Southern Alberta Japanese Canadians.* Lethbridge, AB: Graphcom Printers.

Nakagama, K. (2005-2010). Personal communication.

Nippon Steel Human Resources Development Company Limited. (1988). *Nippon: The land and its people.* Japan.

Sunahara, A.G. (1981). *The politics of racism: The uprooting of Japanese Canadians during the Second World War.* Toronto: James Lorimer.

Sunahara, A., & Sunahara, D. (1985). The Japanese in Alberta. In H. Palmer, & T. Palmer (Eds.). *Peoples of Alberta: Portraits of cultural diversity* (pp. 394-412). Saskatoon, SK: Western Producer Prairie Books.

Takata, T. (1983). *Nikkei legacy: The story of Japanese Canadians from settlement to today.* Toronto: NC Press.

Tomomitsu, C. (2005). Personal communication.